The Freeway
of Life

The Journey of Driving a Fearless Path

MICHELLE PEAVY

.

DEDICATION

This book is dedicated to my dear friend, Rene.

RIP, my dear friend.

CONTENTS

ACKNOWLEDGMENTS

Thank you to my family for being there (Darcy, Jason, Mom and Dad). Thank you to my eWomenNetwork sisterhood in Canada and the USA. Thank you to my 5 Circles Dream Team who constantly helps me evolve.

i

CHAPTER 1

People ask me all the time. Who are you? What are you? Where did you come from? Where are you going and where are you now? Depending on what day it is right; do you get asked or ask yourself one or all of these same questions too? Come along with me on this journey I call the 'Freeway of Life' and learn just how simply driving your car can answer all these questions.

I want to get a few thank you's out of the way first. I am so incredibly humbled, blessed and grateful for a chance to live life out-loud and in color. To my higher power for granting me the wisdom to change the things I can, and know the difference of the things I cannot. To all my family and friends, you know who you are. Last but not least, the two most fearless women I know, Rene and Marj who changed my life, and inspired me to be aware of my gifts of insight, and to use my gifts.

As I move forward and face each new 'fork in the road', I continue to choose the fearless path. I want to share me with you on my freeway of life, and how I became 'The Final Note'. This journey called life has its ups and downs, but during these times of fear, I for some reason always got back on track and found the blessing at the end of the rainbow. As I walk my personal path, I have come to find my answers along the way.

You will hear me use the words 'Fork in the Road', 'Freeway' and 'Exit', which is the path I walk in life. The fork in the road and exits are the fearless choices and changes I made. The people I met who helped me along the way, and what the outcomes of those decisions were. Some of these are by choice and some were not. The Final Note is myself, delivering a lasting impression and final footprint through the songs and music I sing, to awaken the sleeping giant inside you. I came to the fork in the road and choose the fearless route and so my journey begins.

Where am I going? I want you to take a deep, deep slow breathe and pause with silence, and imagine yourself driving on the freeway, at the speed-limit. You start out at the right speed and eventually it picks up and still you drive even faster. Coffee cup in one hand, cell phone in the other and you even still find a way to change the radio station, and quickly check yourself out in the front mirror.

You now are moving at such a fast speed, that you forget to signal into the next lane to pass the cars in front of you. Not paying attention, you missed your exit sign and have to make a U Turn and go back the same way you just came. You get back on the freeway, start at the regular speed and end up even going faster. This time you hear a large thud! and realize that you have a flat tire. You are completely at a dead stop in the middle of the freeway and cars are driving past you. No one is helping you change your tire, so you call someone to help. You immediately want to cuss and swear as now your schedule has been taken off course, and you sit and wait patiently as you now have no choice and cannot go anywhere until help arrives. Several thoughts and ideas cross through your mind, on what secret magical powers you could draw up to just make the flat tire work again. So frustrated, as you know for sure you will now miss your appointment.

Take another slow deep breathe! Sound familiar? Look familiar? Let me explain, I was on that freeway moving at fast speed, not signaling not paying attention to the signs. Making good money, nice car and nice house; busy, busy, busy. I got off on the wrong exit and then all of a sudden I got a flat tire.

CHAPTER 2

Where did I come from? In 1995 during my move to Houston Texas, I learnt that I had stage three cervical cancer at twenty-nine years old. What? I thought I had a spare in my car to change the flat tire; I was speechless as I was now in an area not familiar to me at all. Fear sets in, no spare tire, ran out of gas, and all of a sudden I came out of my daydreaming state and back to my reality and conversation in my doctor's office.

As a newcomer at that time, I grappled with the American complex medical system, and the toughest fight of all. I went into survival mode and wanted to find the answers, and for it to all just go away. I was so caught up in getting better that I took no time to cry. Feeling sorry for myself and to top it all, I had no female friends or support to console and reassure me that everything would be ok. During this process, I underwent intensive and evasive treatments. For now my hope was temporarily elated. It has taken me fifteen years to actually speak about my cancer and really get in-touch with facing my fear and grieve that person.

For a moment and for the very first time, you will hear in detail, express my inner-most thoughts, as I write a letter to myself, in honor of myself, to heal myself and face my fears; as I begin to fix my flat tire on my own:

Dear God remember me, it is me Michelle. Hello, are you there? I know it has been a long time, how are you? There is something I need to get off my chest and I thought you were the best person to talk to. Do you have a minute to listen? Remember in May of 1995 when I moved to Houston, Texas from Calgary, Alberta? Well I received a phone call from my doctor in Calgary, asking if I could come by her office the next day as she had something to tell me. I replied back to her that I now live in Houston Texas. She shared with me that the information that she needed to give was very personal and that she needed me in her office immediately. What she was about to tell me needed to be done in person. At that point I became very nervous and I could not figure out what was wrong. I booked a plane ticket with all the money I had left and went back to Calgary the next day, drove from the airport to her office thinking we would go through a small conversation, and I would turn around and come right back to Houston Texas. Well, that was not the case. As I walked into my doctor's office, she walked in with a solace look on her face, and she said to me she was not going to sugar-coat anything, and advised I had stage three cervical cancer.

At that moment I was literally shocked. I thought to myself, oh my God! I am only 29 years old this cannot be, it is not true. I asked my doctor to repeat what she said three times, it seemed like an eternity to me. I wanted her to tell me this was a joke, and that she was going to give me a clean bill of health. My head began to spin in circles as I am thinking; I now live in Houston, Texas. I am engaged to get married, and what the heck do I do with this medical issue? I collected all my thoughts and all my medical records and flew back to Houston.

Still not understanding and knowing how the medical system works in the United States and not having any medical insurance, I proceeded to contact the best Cancer Hospital in Houston and they told me it would cost me $5000 to get started. I again was shocked, why do you have to pay to go to the Doctor? What is this all about? Does anyone not care about how I am feeling, and that I have no money, and that I am starting a new life here? Absolutely not! Hello God, are you still there? Are you really listening? Why me? Why do these people want me to pay money to go to the doctor? I am so angry, upset, resentful and frustrated as I did not understand. Please make this all go away.

After praying real hard and contemplating my next move, I decided to enroll myself into a new clinical trial for women who had cervical cancer. The procedure that they were performing would normally demand a one to two months recovery period. I went through so many tests that I felt like a guinea pig, and that I was up for bids to the highest bidder. I had doctors from all around the world staring between my legs, so they could evaluate this new procedure. My surgery and recovery went off without a hitch. I was discharged and the healing now begins right, wrong! My thoughts were, I have uprooted myself from Canada to the United States, sold all my belongings, sold my home and car in Calgary and now I am engaged to be married and have no money left. So broke I could not even afford to buy deodorant. No car to drive and now I have been told that I have cancer. How am I going to get out of this mess? Please God, help me.

How did I get through those days with such sadness, depression and despair? I found a calendar and marked off each day with either a check mark or an x. The check mark was for good days and the x was for bad days. But more than anything God, why can't I have a girlfriend? You see women can give certain things to other women emotionally that a man can't. I took my situation and utilized it to help not only my health issues, but also my emotional and mental state. I was so obsessed with getting better and beating this that I read every self-help book there was out there. I attended workshops, sought counseling from a psychiatrist, psychologist and psychotherapist and took antidepressants to smother the psychosis. I felt like I was buried in a hole that I could not get out of.

Little did I realized, that sometimes God has to put us in a spot, where we cannot move or get out of. So we will pay attention, and the silent whisper speaks to me and said, 'stand still so that others can share their light'. I am so grateful to know I have survived this chapter in my life. I utilized this time to recover, heal and think about just how precious life is.

As a result my recovery process was successful, and back on the freeway I go. I obtained medical insurance, and two months later with my new employer, I volunteered myself to work one hundred percent commission recruiter job. I promised my employer I would become their number one employee, and outlined the projected revenues I would generate for them in seven months. I elected one hundred percent commission, as I was told that I did not have a job when I moved to Houston. My employer accepted my business plan so I could obtain and keep medical insurance. On December 31, 1995 I became one of the top producing recruiters, and that my job would continue on. For the years to come I continued to make the top five producing recruiters in North America. What an accomplishment this was? This gave me time to reflect and rejuvenate my soul and celebrate me. Finally God, thank you, something is finally going right; little did I know it was just for a short time.

From 1995 to 2001, those were the best years of my life. I transitioned from an apartment to a house, no car to a luxury vehicle, corporate job to business owner, travelling around the world buying and having whatever I wanted. It was the beginning of a new chapter in creating a good life, or so I thought. September of 2001, remember the date like it was yesterday. I was told pre-cancerous cells were detected again, and that surgery would be needed to burn the cancer cells. I asked myself is this really true? I thought I was driving the speed limit on the freeway. I was doing all the right things, signaling and obeying the road signs. But what I came to realize, was that I was driving on the wrong freeway, going the wrong way and did not even know it. I felt like someone had hit me from behind. How come I did not see it coming, what is going to happen to me again, am I going to die? At this point in my career I had just left my corporate job and opened up my own recruiting business, but I got caught in between. I was denied individual medical coverage until the cancer was taken care of, and as a result I had to pay over $14,000 to have surgery. I was one of those middle class professionals who was denied health insurance but did not have enough money to have the surgery.

Sometimes things just eventually work themselves out, as I seem to reroute myself, and get back on the freeway going in the right direction. As I learnt the ropes of running a recruiting business and how to change my own flat tire, I became more self-aware that only I have the choice to change and accept the things I can, and let go of the things I can't. The success of my recruiting business and the people around it completely boosted my ego with praise, affirmation, recognition and attention on a daily basis. By changing my state of mind and surrendering and accepting what happen to me, the universe seemed to give back to me what I put out there. The cancer was now old news and the stresses in my life became different.

You see at times we are standing at the edge of the cliff, which represents us having to make difficult decisions. At first we think, if I jump or make the wrong decision, I am going to fall. What you need to realize is one of two things will happen if you jump and make a decision; either someone will catch you or you will learn how to fly. So what is stopping you from making that decision or change in your life? Did you fall, are you flying or did someone catch you.

Cancer has given me the courage to look at myself, and really face my fears and find out what I am made of. I hope that everyone who listens to my story chooses in helping to support their own charitable organization, and a portion of the proceeds from my books and CD support mine. This was not easy for me to write, as my emotions got all stirred up, and I relive those days all over again. I guess I did not realize how much I went through, and what one woman can be and that this will not be my final stop. I now know that I can change and fix my own flat tire, and always know that if I miss my exit signs, I can always get off at the next one. Usually, I am pleasantly surprised what I find along the way, even when it is not familiar to me.

We have so much power and underestimate how we can use it. You and I are holding the key. Take that key and continue to unlock all those doors inside you. What door will you choose to unlock and free yourself? When I went through cancer the first time I was focused on getting better. The second time, I was determined to fight it and have it never to come back again. It is so amazing how free I felt when I wrote this letter to myself. I cried like a baby for three days, as I did not realize that this door needed to be unlocked, and then the person came out to hear herself. Life does not stand still, we must pay it forward and teach others what we know and be the change. Share your story out-loud, you don't know who it will help. Brush the dirt off get back on that freeway, drive the speed limit and even if you get off on the wrong exit, enjoy the place you are in at that moment. Be the change. I got it now, I can help others.

CHAPTER 3

They say that the ones who go through the most pain and tragedy turns out to be the best teachers. All that I have gone through was no mistake, this was all planned accordingly to lead me to where I am today. I now have the strength to bless and help others find their gift of insight. Listen carefully; come closer as I tell you more about the DETOUR I took off the freeway. In 2008 my dearest friend, self-employed for nineteen years had a heart attack on a sales call. Not knowing she was having a heart attack she went home and fell asleep, thinking she would feel better when she woke up. Little did she know what was about to happen. She went into diabetic coma; sugar went to 900, lost her eyesight and mobility and had open heart surgery. She was in comatose state for four days not knowing if she would make it. As the days went by, she began to gain her strength back, but learning to deal with her medical state and not being able to see, was a huge transition and reprogramming of the mind. She was my neighbor at that time and I would go over to her house and massage her feet, buy groceries and food to help accommodate the huge financial burden it took to keep the household running. I cannot even imagine what she was going through, but I do look back at what the blessing was out of this. You see when someone is blind they gain intuitive abilities and can read the energy of a person. That has always been inspiring so to me and something I call a blessing and gift. Fast forward, eighteen eye surgeries later to regain her eyesight as well as a living a holistic lifestyle, she regained her eyesight and mobility. Can she lead the same lifestyle as before? Maybe. Does she have the same choices as before? Possibly. You see when you have gone through a traumatic lifestyle change your choices become different. You appreciate what really matters to you and take nothing for granted. Don't wait to make a change in your life when you do not have a choice anymore. Live your dreams and passions when you can. On July 14, 2014 my dear friend went home to be with the Lord and no longer is suffering the burden of these illnesses. She is now in a state of pure peace, happiness and joy and I continue to share her light with you.

Recalculating route, fasten seatbelt check, lights turned on check, car now is in drive check, GPS on check, ready set go. I am now back on the freeway, recalculating route, recalculating route. Wait a second; I am almost sure I am at the right place, not this time.

December 28, 2008 my other close friend was training for a triathlon and was on her weekly bike run with her group, when all of a sudden from out of nowhere, she was hit by a car from behind at sixty miles an hour. She was ejected into the air, and was thrown like a rag doll. She landed on the ground forward on her neck and was immediately paralyzed and is now a quadriplegic. Her helmet saved her life. That was two close friends of mine in three months. Am I next? I lived with such anxiety and pressure to run her medical business and personal affairs until her family could get acclimated to the medical jargons in the United States and Canada. I became the mediator, negotiator, peacemaker debater between her family, doctors, lawyers, employers, to find peace.

For a total of six months she went through intensive rehab in order for the doctors to even look at her the same way again. As tragic as this may seem my friend shared something with me that is so powerful that I repeat it to myself every day. She said don't feel sorry for me because I cannot use my arms and legs, 'there are many people out there who have the use of their arms and legs and are more disabled than I am', how powerful is that.

Where am I now? After all is said and done, little did I know that the trials, tribulation and tragedies were the experiences which became the gift. After every rainstorm there is a rainbow at the end. This I call the gift of insight, choose to see all the colors of the rainbow.

In life there are times when we are stripped naked to be completely exposed, and then we build ourselves up again. Think of the time when you have been there, what is the gift of insight? What are the colors of the rainbow did you see? As we continue to travel on our freeway of life, we will be forever choosing our forks in the road, always looking for our final destination.

So when someone asks you now, you should answer with the following. I came to the fork in the road and choose the fearless route, and so my journey begins and on that final note.

MICHELLE PEAVY

THE FINAL WRITTEN NOTE

Life is an Empty Space. What are you going to choose to fill it up with? As I look in the rear view mirror and see the freeway behind me, it is always a small reminder to understand life backwards, so I could learn how to navigate moving forward.

After several years of staying stuck in my story, I woke up and decided it's my choice to create this amazing life as I slowly picked myself back up piece by piece. New people came into my life that grabbed my hand and nudged me with compassion, love and support and pulled me higher and higher. Many times I did not have the answers, fearful of failing, but I found myself continuing to move forward as I checked in to re-evaluate my circles of influence and move forward with action, saying YES to making peace in my life. No more judgment, fault, blame. I created healthy relationships in all forms, but the most important one that needed the nurturing was myself. From there nothing but results started to appear.

We spend so much time on the freeway, driving the same route, staying in the same lane, at the same speed, and wont speed up and pass the vehicles ahead of us. But this time, I welcome the detours with the opportunity to choose new exits off the freeway. It's just another way to see the road in a different way.

What's next? Welcome to the world as I breathe new oxygen and life to the 5 Circles of Influence Mastermind Experiences,. The opportunity to serve others by showing them how to tap into their VOICE by connecting them through my database/network to further identify, evaluate and create their very own Dream team.

Here's to connecting the dots and drawing the circles.

For more information, please go to www.michellepeavy.com

ABOUT THE AUTHOR

MICHELLE PEAVY

Michelle Peavy is described as a multi-dimensional – charismatic motivational speaker, a dynamic singer, and a successful businesswoman in the oil/gas executive recruiting industry (*RimiPV.com*). Her story is inspirational: She is a Cancer Thriver. She is a courageous woman. After taking a sabbatical in her business life, she decided to travel across North America telling her story and inspiring others to live a fearless life – and to understand everything that happens, the good, the bad and as described in her own words, "I came to the fork in the road and chose the fearless route and so my journey begins."

Michelle assisted in Writing/Producing/Authoring her first CD, and her own book, and shares her story about her journey on the FREEWAY OF LIFE.

In addition, she is the creator, and facilitator of the 5 Circles of Influence Mastermind Experience Workshops throughout Canada and the United States

Amongst all these talents, Michelle created her amazing journey as an inspirational speaker in North America at events, such as, eWomenNetwork, Canadian Center for Abuse Awareness, Business of Bliss, Fearless Women's Day, ALLWomen Summit, Courageous Living, Braveheart Women, Brilliant Minded Women, and can be seen singing the National Anthem for the NBA Houston Rockets and NBA Allstar Weekend and performing as a Salsa Dancer.

To learn more about Michelle and to connect further, please visit her personal website at **MichellePeavy.com.**

Made in the USA
Charleston, SC
17 September 2014